# Energy

**Ashley Lee**

Explore other books at:
WWW.ENGAGEBOOKS.COM

VANCOUVER, B.C.

e→ WWW.ENGAGEBOOKS.COM

*Energy: Level 2*
*I Can Help Save Earth!*
Lee, Ashley 1995 –
Text © 2021 Engage Books
Design © 2021 Engage Books

Edited by: A.R. Roumanis

Text set in Arial Regular.
Chapter headings set in Arial Black.

FIRST EDITION / FIRST PRINTING

LIBRARY AND ARCHIVES CANADA CATALOGUING IN PUBLICATION

Title: Energy: I Can Help Save Earth Level 2
Names: Lee, Ashley, 1995- author

Identifiers: Canadiana (print) 20200309862 | Canadiana (ebook) 20200309870
ISBN 978-1-77437-722-2 (hardcover)
ISBN 978-1-77437-723-9 (softcover)
ISBN 978-1-77437-724-6 (pdf)
ISBN 978-1-77437-725-3 (epub)
ISBN 978-1-77437-726-0 (kindle)

Subjects:
LCSH: Power resources—Environmental aspects—Juvenile literature
LCSH: Environmental protection—Citizen participation—Juvenile literature

Classification: LCC TJ163.23 .L44 2020 | DDC J333.79—DC23

# Contents

4   What is Energy?

6   How is Energy Made?

8   Why is Energy Important?

10  Energy Around the World

12  What is Energy Pollution?

14  Are All Kinds of
      Energy Harmful?

16  Energy Pollution Facts

18  How Energy Pollution
      Affects Animals

20  How Energy Pollution
      Affects Humans

22  How Energy Pollution
      Affects Earth

24  Energy Conservation

26  Reducing Energy Pollution

28  The Future of Energy

30  Quiz

## What is Energy?

Energy is another word for power. Light bulbs, cars, and computers all need energy to work.

People use energy every day. It helps to make our lives easier and safer.

# How is Energy Made?

The most common way to make energy is by burning **fossil fuels**. There are only so many fossil fuels on Earth. Once they are gone, we will not have any more.

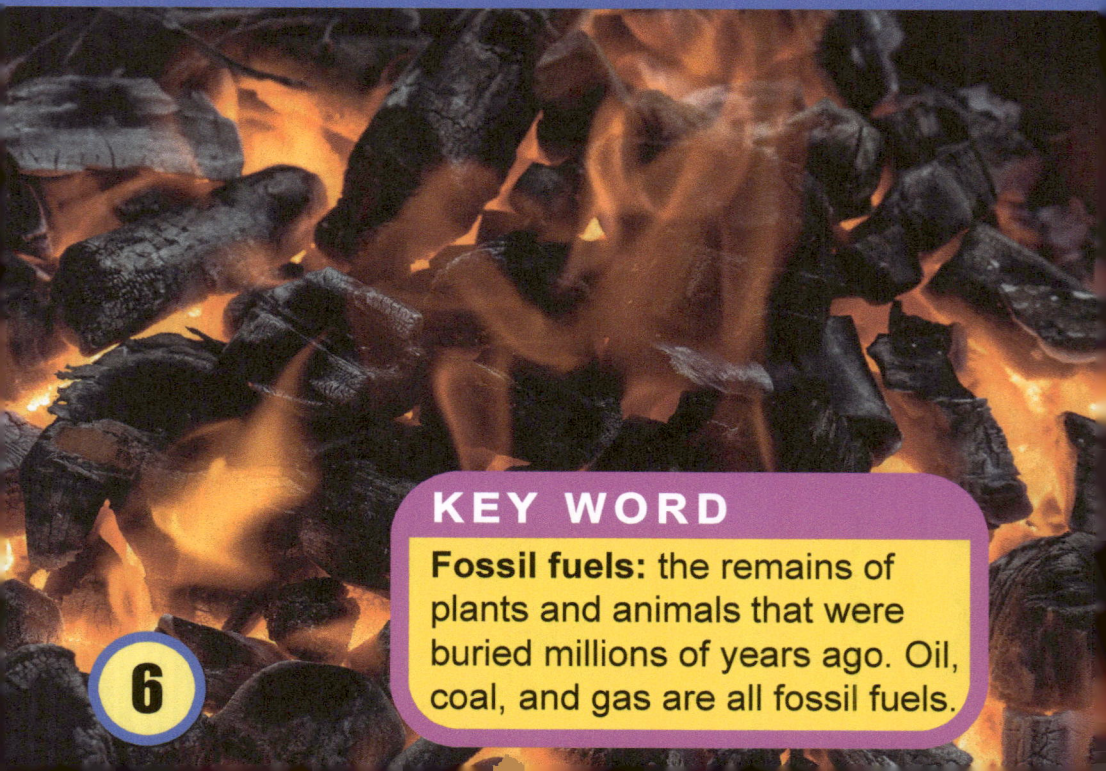

**KEY WORD**

**Fossil fuels:** the remains of plants and animals that were buried millions of years ago. Oil, coal, and gas are all fossil fuels.

Some kinds of energy are renewable. This means they come from sources that will never disappear. Solar power uses the Sun to create energy. Hydropower creates energy using moving water. Wind power is energy created by the wind.

## Why is Energy Important?

Energy makes all technology work. Medical equipment is a type of technology that can help save people's lives.

Energy also creates heat so people can cook food and stay warm. This is very important in cold places around the world.

## Energy Around the World

The Unites States, China, and India use more fossil fuels than any other country. Iceland uses the most renewable energy. About 90% of their energy comes from renweable sources.

The Gansu Wind Farm in China is the largest wind farm in the world. One of the largest solar power plants is the Noor Power Station in Morocco. The Gharwar oil field in Saudi Arabia is the largest oil field in the world.

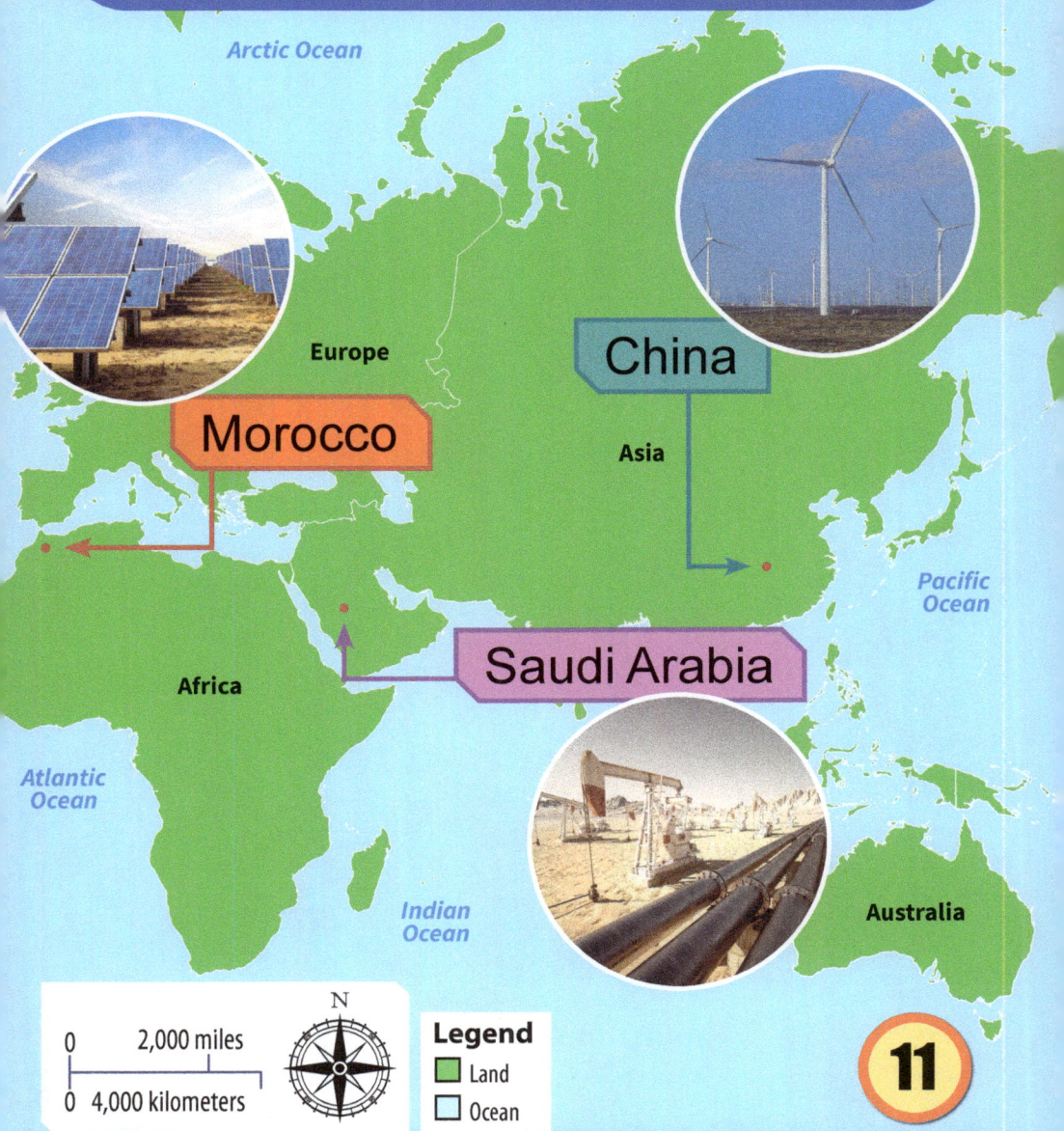

Arctic Ocean

Europe

China

Morocco

Asia

Africa

Saudi Arabia

Atlantic Ocean

Indian Ocean

Pacific Ocean

Australia

0    2,000 miles

0    4,000 kilometers

N

Legend
Land
Ocean

11

# What is Energy Pollution?

Pollution is when chemicals or waste enter the **environment**. Some kinds of energy pollute the air. This means harmful chemicals are released into the air when energy is created.

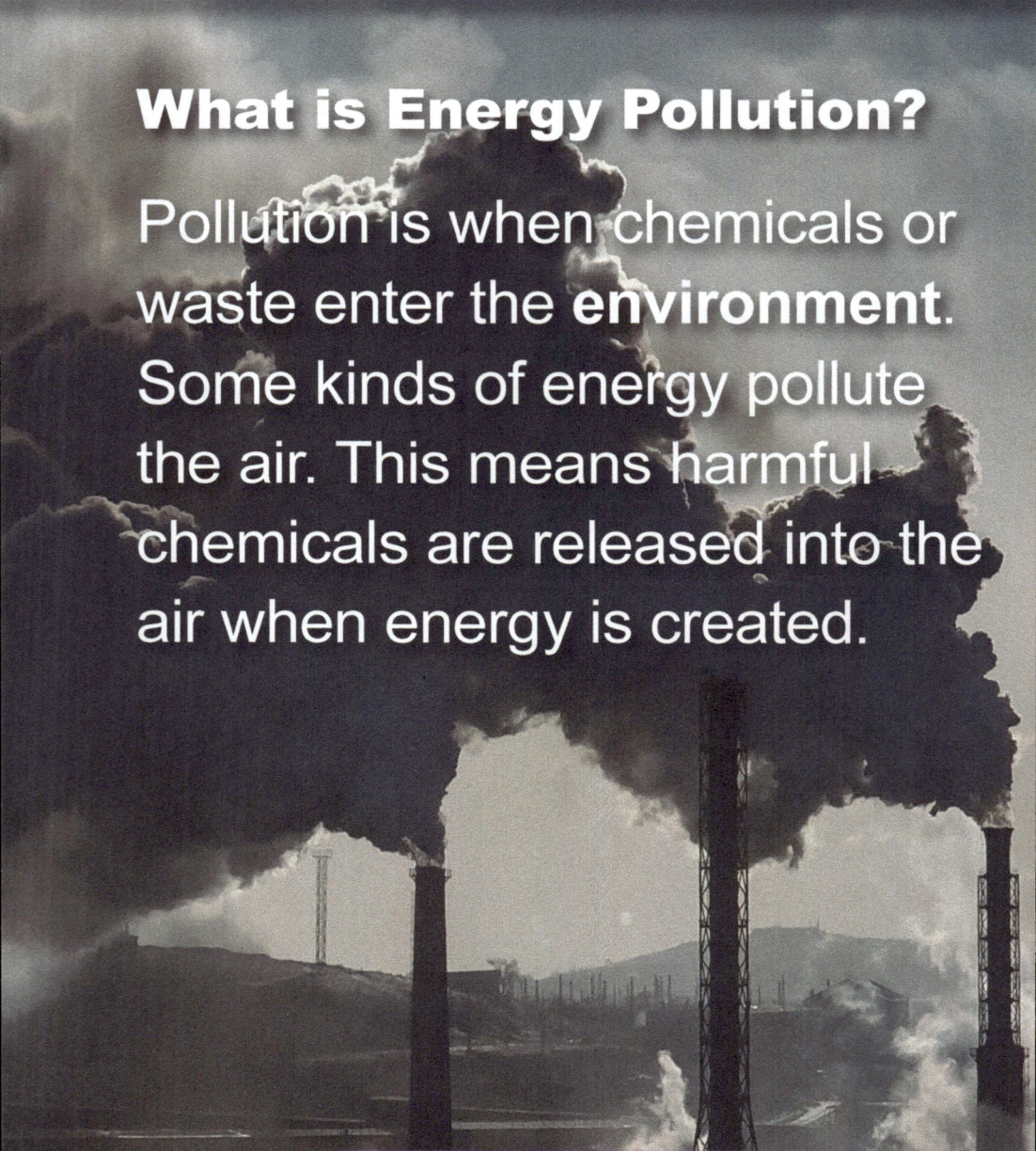

**KEY WORD**

**Environment:** places around Earth that include living and non living things.

Some companies use water to cool down the steam produced by burning fossil fuels. Companies then put this water back into rivers or oceans. The water that is returned is often harmful to animals and humans.

## Are All Kinds of Energy Harmful?

Solar power, hydropower, and wind power are kinds of clean energy. This means they do not pollute Earth.

14

Fossil fuels need to be dug up from the ground. This can cause chemicals to leak into water sources and animal habitats. Burning fossil fuels also creates air pollution.

15

# Energy Pollution Facts

About eighty percent of Earth's energy is created by burning fossil fuels.

Over 4.9 million barrels of oil were spilled into the ocean while digging up oil in the Gulf of Mexico in 2010.

Around 12.6 million Americans breathe in air pollution from fossil fuels every day.

16

It would take more than 400 years for Earth to replace all the fossil fuels the world uses in one year.

It takes about 800 pounds (362 kilograms) of coal to power a lightbulb for an entire year without turning it off.

Health problems caused by burning fossil fuels costs the world about $8 billion every day.

## How Energy Pollution Affects Animals

Animal habitats are destroyed when fossil fuels are dug up from the earth. Large areas of forests and mountains are destroyed to reach the ground underneath.

18

If animals are able to find a new home, they have to compete for food with the other animals already living there.

# How Energy Pollution Affects Humans

Breathing in polluted air can make people very sick. Air pollution can harm people's lungs, heart, kidneys, brain, and blood.

Sometimes gas will leak from a power plant. This causes lots of chemicals to enter the air at once. When this happens, people are forced to **evacuate** their homes to stay safe.

**KEY WORD**

**Evacuate:** when people have to leave their homes and communities for safety reasons.

# How Energy Pollution Affects Earth

Air pollution is one of the causes of global warming. Global warming means Earth's temperature is rising. This happens when chemicals become trapped in Earth's **atmosphere**.

**KEY WORD**

**Atmosphere:** a layer of gas that surrounds Earth. It provides air for living things to breathe.

Global warming causes extreme weather. These are things like hurricanes and tornadoes. There will be more extreme weather as Earth gets warmer.

# Energy Conservation

Energy conservation means using less energy. The less energy people use, the less pollutants are released into the air. Here are some ways to save energy at home.

Unplug electronics when they are not being used.

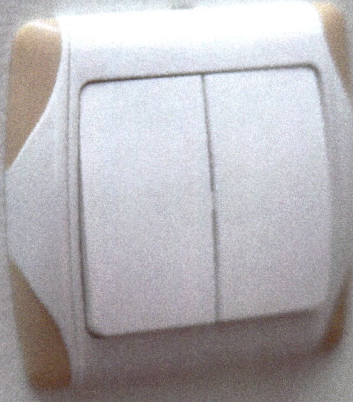

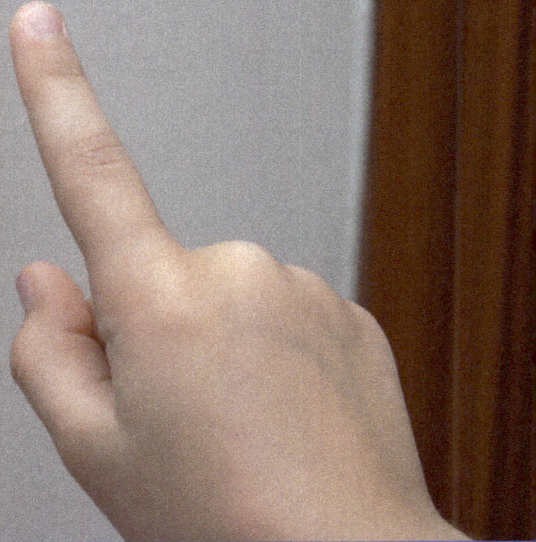

Turn off the lights
when no one is in
a room.

Take shorter showers.

## Reducing Energy Pollution

Some companies are creating lights, heaters, and electronics that do not use as much energy to work. This can help reduce energy pollution and lower household energy bills.

Many household items can be replaced with ones that do not use as much energy.

**Lightbulb**  **LED lightbulb**

**Wall outlet**  **Power Strip**

**Air conditioner**  **Ceiling fan**

## The Future of Energy

Many countries are switching to using clean energy. Sweden has challenged the rest of the world to a race to use clean energy sources for everything.

Sweden mainly uses solar and wind power. They plan to use only clean energy sources by the year 2040.

# Quiz

Test your knowledge of energy by answering the following questions. The questions are based on what you have read in this book. The answers are listed on the bottom of the next page.

**1** What is the most common way to make energy?

**2** What does it mean if energy is renewable?

**3** What is destroyed when fossil fuels are dug up?

**4** What does global warming mean?

**5** What is energy conservation?

**6** What two kinds of energy does Sweden mainly use?

# Explore other level 2 readers.

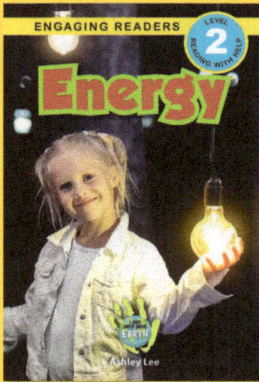

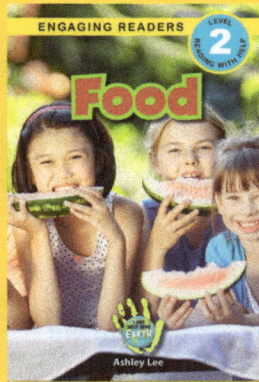

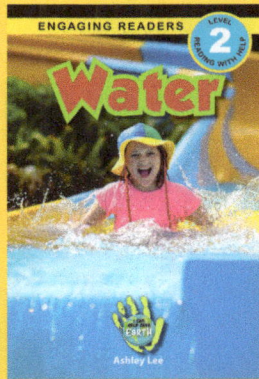

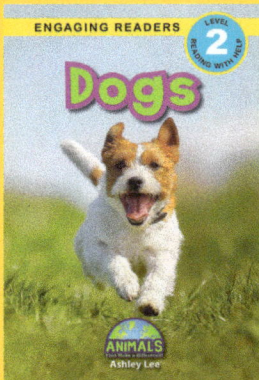

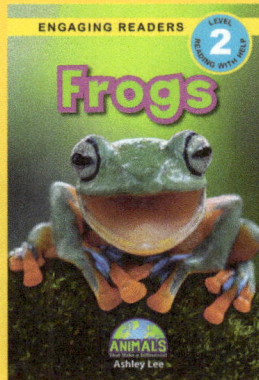

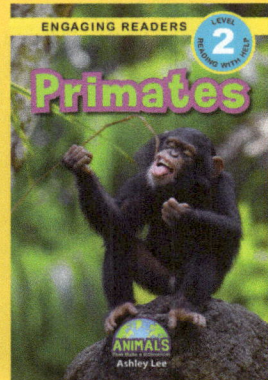

Visit www.engagebooks.com to explore more Engaging Readers.

Answers: 1. Burning fossil fuels 2. It comes form sources that will never disappear 3. Animal habitats 4. Earth's temperature is rising 5. Using less energy 6. Solar and wind power

www.ingramcontent.com/pod-product-compliance
Lightning Source LLC
Chambersburg PA
CBHW051236020426
42331CB00016B/3397